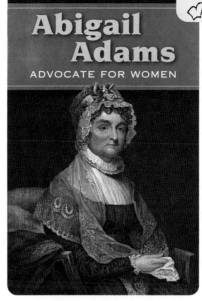

Abigail Adams
ADVOCATE FOR WOMEN

Tammy Orr Staats

Boston, Massachusetts
Chandler, Arizona
Glenview, Illinois
Upper Saddle River, New Jersey

Illustrations

2, 4, 5, 6, 10, 12, 14 Norbert Sipos.

Photographs

Every effort has been made to secure permission and provide appropriate credit for photographic material.
The publisher deeply regrets any omission and pledges to correct errors called to its attention in subsequent editions.

Unless otherwise acknowledged, all photographs are the property of Pearson Education, Inc.

Photo locators denoted as follows: Top (T), Center (C), Bottom (B), Left (L), Right (R), Background (Bkgd)

Opener: Prints and Photographs Division, LC-USZ62-10016/Library of Congress; 1 Prints and Photographs Division, LC-USZ62-10016/Library of Congress; 3 Prints and Photographs Division, LC-DIG-ppmsca-15705/Library of Congress; 7 Detroit Publishing Company Photograph Collection, Prints and Photographs Division, LC-D4-17010/Library of Congress; 8 Prints and Photographs Division, Library of Congress, LC-USZ62-55196; 9 Prints and Photographs Division, LC-USZC2-2243/Library of Congress; 11 Prints and Photographs Division, LC-USZC4-4970/Library of Congress; 13 Prints and Photographs Division, Library of Congress, LC-USZC2-2645; 15 Prints and Photographs Division, LC-USZ62-10016/Library of Congress.

ISBN-13: 978-0-328-67640-8
ISBN-10: 0-328-67640-3

1 2 3 4 5 6 7 8 9 10 V0FL 15 14 13 12 11

A Remarkable Woman

Abigail Adams lived at a time when women had few choices about how they would live their lives. Women were expected to get married, have children, and take care of their families. They could not have a career, vote, or run for office. They had no say in government.

Abigail Adams and other girls of her time learned just enough math to pay bills and manage a household. They learned to read and spell so they could read the Bible and write letters. They were not expected to **influence** world affairs. In fact, being too well educated was thought to be an obstacle to finding a husband. Many men did not want a wife with too much education.

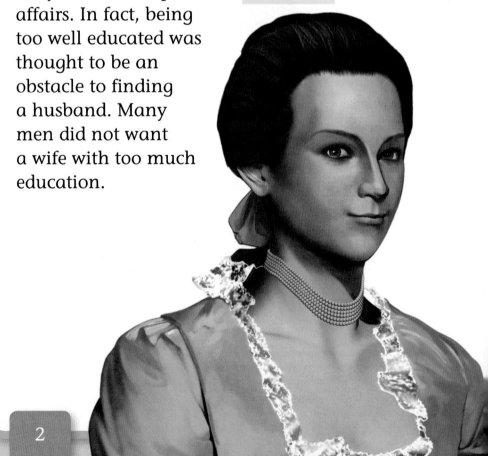

Despite these limits, Abigail Adams became a very well-educated woman. She was an **advocate**, or supporter, of women's rights. She helped shape the course of history by advising her husband John Adams, the second president of the United States. She also had great

John Adams

influence on her son, John Quincy Adams, who became our sixth president.

Abigail wrote hundreds of letters during her lifetime. They show her views and give us a fascinating look at what life was like during some of the country's important early events. They also show the closeness between Abigail Adams and her husband.

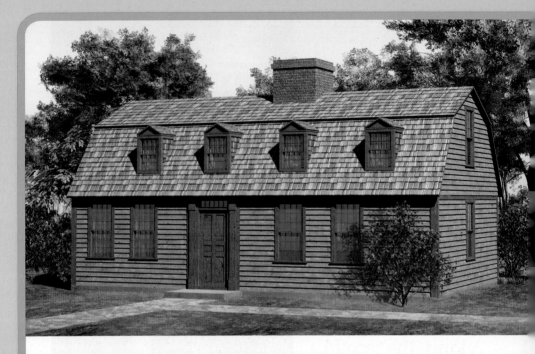

Growing Up

Abigail Adams was born Abigail Smith on November 11, 1744, in Weymouth, Massachusetts. She was the second of four children. Her father, William Smith, served as the minister in Weymouth. At that time, ministers were often the most educated men in town.

As was the custom, Abigail Smith was taught at home by her mother. However, her father's library was available to her. William Smith encouraged all of his children to share his love of learning. Thanks to her father's library, Abigail Smith had educational opportunities that most girls of her time did not. She studied as many different subjects as she could.

Education

Even though Abigail read a lot, she had poor spelling and grammar skills that embarrassed her all her life. Fortunately, she did not allow her embarrassment to keep her from writing. Thanks to her letters, we know a great deal about her.

Adams always regretted that she had not gone to school as boys did. In her letters she often expressed the wish that things would change for women. She wanted women to have the same opportunities for education as men. In one letter she wrote, "You need not be told how much female education is **neglected**."

John Adams

In 1762, a young lawyer by the name of John Adams began spending time with Abigail Smith. They fell in love.

The couple lived only five miles from each other and saw each other often. However, they still wrote many letters during the two years they courted. They got to know each other very well.

The letters of both were filled with warmth and respect. For Abigail, writing letters was a way to express her thoughts and feelings. She once wrote, "My pen is always freer than my tongue. I have wrote many things to you that I suppose I never could have talked."

John Adams was born in this house in 1735.

Marriage

Abigail Smith and John Adams were married on October 25, 1764. It was the beginning of a partnership that would last 54 years.

The couple settled at John's childhood home in Braintree, Massachusetts. It was not long before John Adams became a very important leader in the American **colonies**, which were ruled by Great Britain. Because of his work, the two were apart for months or even years at a time. Because of these long absences, we have hundreds of letters recording their thoughts and commenting on the events of the time.

Boston

In 1768, John and Abigail Adams moved to Boston to be closer to John Adams's work. Abigail Adams loved living in the bustling city. She was kept busy raising her growing family. She had three children now. She also had a steady stream of interesting visitors, plenty of newspapers

British troops fired on a mob of protestors.

to read, and plenty to talk about. Tensions between the colonies and Britain were rising, and the threat of war was very real.

On March 5, 1770, British troops fired on an angry crowd who were protesting British taxes. Several people were killed. John Adams did not agree with the taxes either, but he defended the British soldiers in court. The public was outraged. However, John Adams felt that every person deserves a fair trial. He also wanted to prove that the colonies were ruled by law, not angry crowds. Abigail Adams supported him through this very difficult time.

Off to Philadelphia

As tensions grew, the colonies moved closer to war with Britain. John Adams was elected to be a **delegate** to the Continental Congress in Philadelphia. The delegates to the congress planned for the colonies' **independence**. They wanted to decide how the country would be governed when the British were no longer in charge.

Like her husband, Abigail Adams supported independence. She knew it was John Adams's duty to go to Philadelphia, but she missed him terribly while he was gone. It was a great **sacrifice** to let him go.

John Adams (right) served on a committee to write the Declaration of Independence.

Apart

While John Adams was away, Abigail Adams returned to Braintree to run the farm and raise their children. What did a wife of the 1770s do when her husband was away for months at a time? In Abigail Adams's case, nearly everything. She hired and managed workers, tended the crops, and milked the cows twice each day. She paid the bills and made the clothes. She did all this while raising and educating the couple's four children, all without dishwashers, laundry machines, or frozen foods. It's amazing she had time to sit down and write so many long letters!

During their time apart, Abigail and John Adams continued to exchange letters. She told him the news from the Boston area. Many of the colonists were **boycotting**, or refusing to buy, British goods. This meant many supplies such as candles, lamp oil, tea, and coffee were **scarce**.

In April 1775, the first battle of the American Revolution was fought in the village of Lexington, Massachusetts. This was just 20 miles away from Braintree. When colonists fought the British a month later on Breed's Hill north of Boston, Abigail and eight-year-old John Quincy raced to the

In one of her letters, Abigail Adams told how she watched a battle from a hill in Braintree.

top of a nearby hill. They could see the flashes of fire and smoke from the battle.

Besides telling the news in her letters, Abigail Adams also gave her opinions. One of her most famous letters was dated March 31, 1776. In the letter she encouraged her husband and the other Congress delegates to "remember the ladies" when they wrote new laws. She warned, "Do not put such unlimited power into the hands of the husbands. Remember all men would be **tyrants** if they could."

Speaking Out

Abigail did not argue only for women's rights. She also felt strongly that **slavery**, which was practiced then in all the colonies, was wrong. "It always appeared a most evil scheme to me," she wrote of slavery. How could some Americans fight for freedom while they enslaved other people? "We are daily robbing and stealing from those who have as good a right to freedom as we have."

Unfortunately, Abigail Adams's wishes for women and enslaved people did not come true in her life time. It would be almost 90 years before slavery and 150 years before women were allowed to vote. However, Abigail Adams spoke out early for these kinds of changes.

More Sacrifices

Later, Congress sent John Adams to France to talk with leaders there. He took their oldest son, John Quincy, with him. It was very hard for Abigail Adams to let them go. It was a dangerous trip. If British ships caught John Adams, he could have been hanged for **treason**. While they were gone, Abigail Adams once more struggled to manage the farm and care for her family. She knew she must sacrifice for her country.

The war ended in 1783. The United States was now an independent country. John Adams continued to serve the nation, first as vice president and then as president himself. He continued to rely on his wife's advice. In 1797, when he became president of the United States, he wrote, "I never wanted your advice and assistance more in my life." He anxiously waited for her to join him.

George Washington is shown here being sworn in as president. John Adams stands to his left.

Mrs. President

We know from John Adams's letters how much he valued Abigail's opinions and advice. However, not everyone shared his admiration of her. Some of President Adams's rivals referred to Abigail Adams as "Mrs. President." They felt she had too much influence over his decisions. Abigail Adams saw no reason not to advise her husband as she had always done. Women may not be able to run the government, she said, but they could still offer their opinions on how men ran it.

The Adamses were the first family to live in the White House. They moved in before it was completely finished.

Home at Last

After John Adams's time as president ended, the couple returned to the farm in Braintree. Finally, they had time together. Abigail Adams enjoyed being near her many grandchildren. She

continued to write letters. She often gave advice to her son, John Quincy. He later became the country's sixth president.

On October 28, 1818, Abigail died of typhoid fever. After she died, John Adams said, "I wish I could lay down beside her and die too."

For the good of her country, Abigail Adams made many sacrifices. She served with courage in many ways. She used her pen to speak out for women's rights and against slavery. She used her brilliant mind to help shape our country's history and to make a difference.

Glossary

advocate a supporter

boycott to refuse to do business with a company or country

colony a place ruled by another country

delegate a person chosen to speak for others

independence freedom from another country's rule

influence the ability to have an effect on others

neglect to ignore

sacrifice something a person gives up

scarce hard to get

slavery the practice of forcing people to work without pay and without freedom

treason the act of being a traitor to one's country

tyrant a ruler with unlimited power who acts cruelly